Make It Yourself

Models

W

This edition published in 2006 by
Franklin Watts
338 Euston Road
London NW1 3BH

Franklin Watts Australia
Hachette Children's Books
Level 17/207 Kent Street
Sydney NSW 2000

Originally published by
Casterman, Belgium
Original edition © Casterman 2002
English edition © Franklin Watts 2006

Projects and text: Lillo Greco
Design: Dominique Mazy
Colour: Véronique Lux
Translation: Ruth Thomson

ISBN-10: 0 7496 6906 3
ISBN-13: 978 0 7496 6906 5

A CIP catalogue record for this book is
available from the British Library.

Dewey Classification: 745.5928

Printed in China

contents

Before you start

About this book

You will find all sorts of fun projects for making models in this book. Every project is simple to make, using easy-to-find materials. You can make a mini-game, a funny person or a useful photo-holder. You can also create lots of different vehicles including a racing car, a boat, a fire engine, a plane, a hot air balloon and a space shuttle.

Once you have learned the basic steps to model-making, try making other models of your own.

Tools and materials

You will need white or coloured card for most of the projects, which you can find in a pad. You will also need empty plastic bottles, cardboard boxes, yogurt pots, corks and the cardboard from rolls of foil or paper towels.

You will need paints and a paintbrush for many of the projects. Gouache paints are the best, because they are thick, dry fast and cover well. Most projects require a pencil, a ruler, scissors and glue or sticky tape. All the materials you will need are listed at the start of each project.

Sizes and measurements

Some projects contain guides for you to follow. The measurements are approximate and sizes may need adjusting according to the materials you use.

It is important that you work to scale. The materials can vary but standard sized plastic bottles and rolls of cardboard from kitchen towels have been used in this book.

Where given the measurements for each design are in centimetres. You can use a ruler to check your designs are accurate before cutting out them out.

Learning logos

The activities in the book provide practice in different skills, identified by the logos below.

An activity practising imagination and creativity

An activity practising fine motor control

An activity involving the notion of balance

An activity practising spatial skills

aquarium

cardboard box ● scissors ● white card ● pencil ● glue
modelling clay ● blue and grey paper ● sticky tape
felt-tip pens or crayons ● thread ● 4 wooden skewers

1 Cut the lid off a cardboard box.

Glue blue paper on to the sides and top of the box, both inside and out. Decorate it with waves.

Rocky seabed scene

2 Glue grey paper on to the box base. Draw and cut out a rocky seabed scene on more grey paper. Glue it around the inside of the box.

Shape rocks from modelling clay. Put them into the box.

3 Draw some fish on to some white card. Colour them and cut them out.

Cut some short lengths of thread. Tape one end on to the back of the fish. Make a loop at the other end of the thread. Repeat for each fish.

4 Pierce four holes on both sides of the box (near the top). Slide in four skewers, slotting them through the loops of thread attached to the fish.

Fix the skewers into the holes on the opposite side of the box.

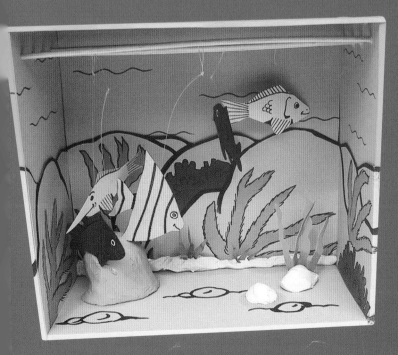

catamaran

2 empty plastic bottles with lids ● gouache paints
paintbrush ● 3 strips of wood ● glue ● cork
white paper ● wooden skewer ● ruler ● scissors

1 Pour half a cup of yellow paint into two plastic bottles.

Screw on the lids. Shake each bottle until the paint has completely coated the inside.

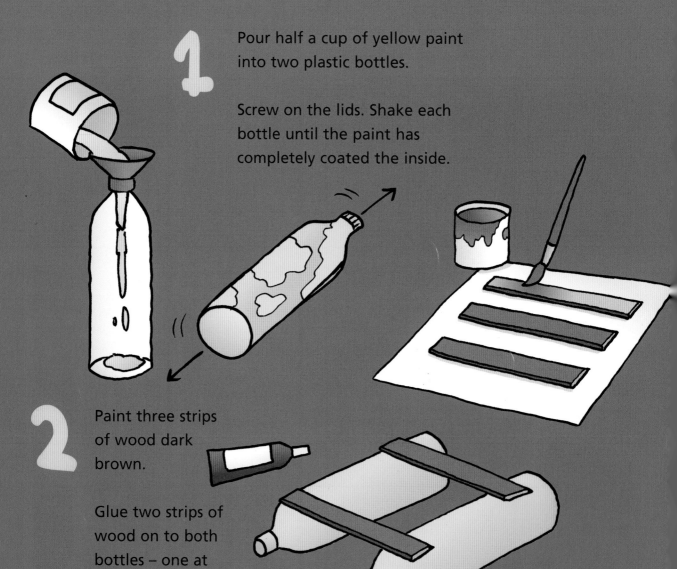

2 Paint three strips of wood dark brown.

Glue two strips of wood on to both bottles – one at either end.

3 Push a skewer into a cork. Glue the cork on to the centre of the third strip of wood. Cut out a small and a large sail from white paper, to the sizes shown below. Paint the large sail.

Use the skewer as a mast and glue the small sail around it. Fit the tip of the large sail over the mast. Glue the other two corners under the strip of wood.

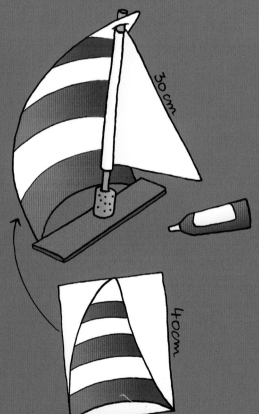

30 cm

40cm

30cm

4 Glue the strip with the mast on to the catamaran, in between the other two strips. Make a small flag. Glue it around the top of the mast.

Space Shuttle

empty plastic bottle with lid ● white gouache paint
paintbrush ● cardboard roll ● white card ● pencil
ruler ● scissors ● crayons or felt-tip pens ● glue

1 Pour half a cup of white paint into a plastic bottle. Screw on the lid. Shake the bottle, until the paint has completely coated the inside.

Cut a cardboard roll into two for the jet engines. Paint both halves white.

2 Cut out two wings and a tail fin from white card, in the sizes shown. Fold up the long edge of both wings and the short end of the tail fin.

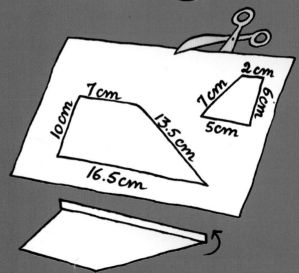

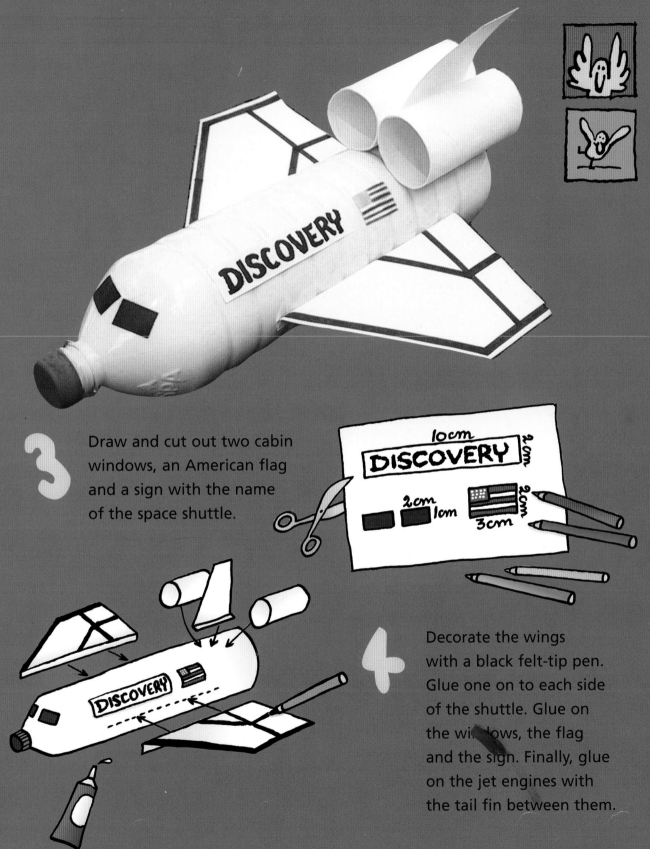

3 Draw and cut out two cabin windows, an American flag and a sign with the name of the space shuttle.

10cm

DISCOVERY

2cm

2cm
1cm

2cm
3cm

4 Decorate the wings with a black felt-tip pen. Glue one on to each side of the shuttle. Glue on the windows, the flag and the sign. Finally, glue on the jet engines with the tail fin between them.

DISCOVERY

DISCOVERY

13

Mini-billiards

empty pizza box ● scissors ● green gouache paint
paintbrush ● 4 plastic cups ● glue ● 2 wooden sticks
thick black felt-tip pen ● 5 ping-pong balls

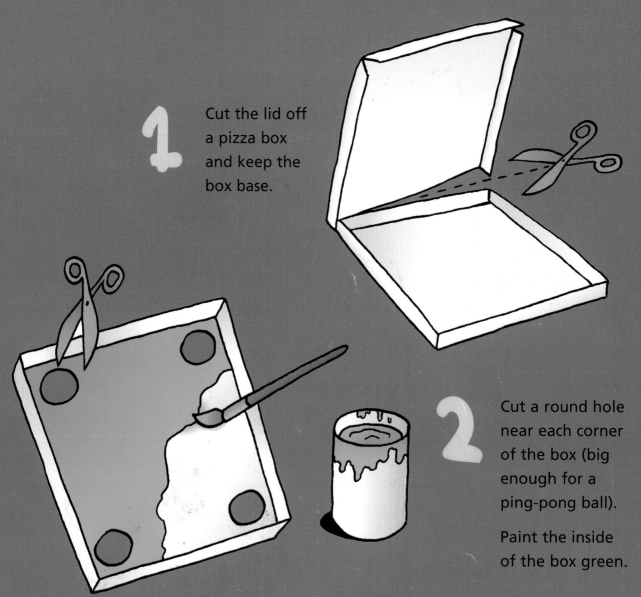

1 Cut the lid off a pizza box and keep the box base.

2 Cut a round hole near each corner of the box (big enough for a ping-pong ball).

Paint the inside of the box green.

3 Cut an opening in the side of four plastic cups (big enough to take out the ping-pong balls). Glue the rim of the cups on to the underside of the box, over each of the holes.

4 Write numbers on five ping-pong balls with a black felt-tip pen.

Use the wooden sticks as cues. Can you pot a ball?

caterpillar photo-holder

coloured modelling clay ● knife ● piece of cardboard
soft wire ● pliers ● toothpick

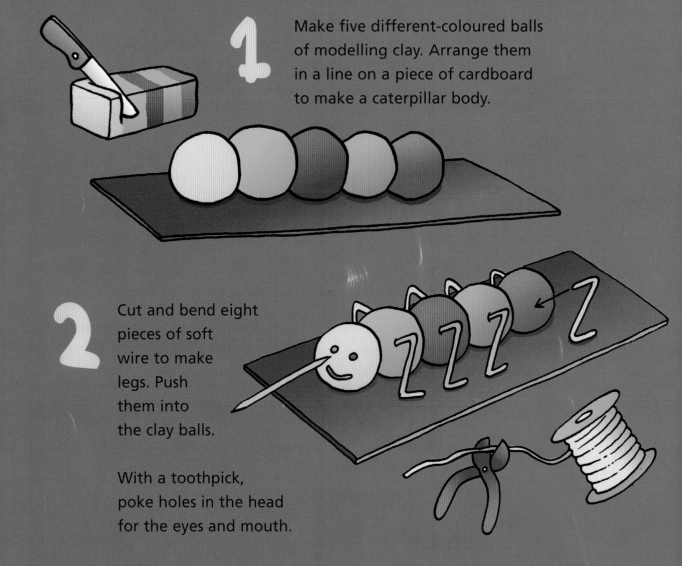

1 Make five different-coloured balls of modelling clay. Arrange them in a line on a piece of cardboard to make a caterpillar body.

2 Cut and bend eight pieces of soft wire to make legs. Push them into the clay balls.

With a toothpick, poke holes in the head for the eyes and mouth.

3 Cut six short pieces of wire and twist the ends to make three pairs of antennae.

4 Push the antennae into alternate balls of clay.

Fix photos into the twisted ends.

balancing man

cardboard roll ● gouache paints ● paintbrush
tracing paper ● pencil ● white card ● scissors
2 empty yogurt pots ● wooden skewer

1 Paint a person – without arms or legs – on to the cardboard roll.

2 Draw some arms and curve templates. Trace and transfer them on to white card. Cut them out.

Paint the arms the same colour as the face, but paint red gloves on the hands.

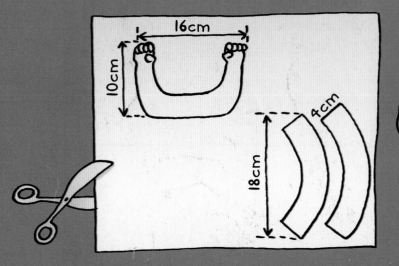

16cm

10cm

18cm

4cm

3 Cut a slit down each shoulder. Cut two parallel slits at the base of the roll on both sides. Slot the arms through the shoulder slits. Slot the two curves into the slits at the base.

Paint legs and feet on the front curve. Snip the top of the roll to make hair.

4 Pierce holes in the man's hands and in both sides of the two yogurt pots, near the top. Slide a wooden skewer through the hands and put a yogurt pot on either end.

Use your balancing man to compare the weight of small objects or keep spare change in it.

Helicopter

empty plastic bottle with lid ● scissors ● gouache paints
● paintbrush ● 2 cardboard rolls ● pencil ● ruler
blue and yellow card ● cork ● strong glue

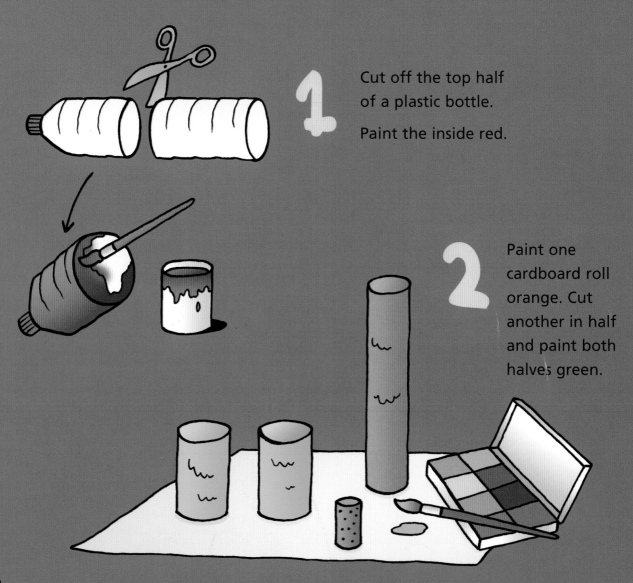

1 Cut off the top half of a plastic bottle.

Paint the inside red.

2 Paint one cardboard roll orange. Cut another in half and paint both halves green.

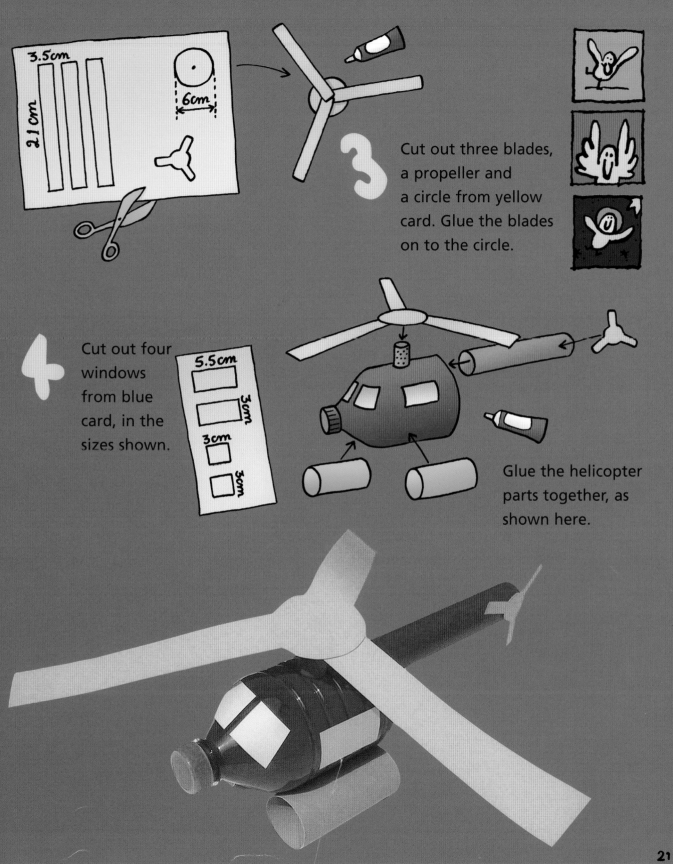

3 Cut out three blades, a propeller and a circle from yellow card. Glue the blades on to the circle.

4 Cut out four windows from blue card, in the sizes shown.

Glue the helicopter parts together, as shown here.

3.5cm
2.1cm
6cm

5.5cm
3cm
3cm
3cm

Hot air balloon

balloon ● newspaper ● flour ● PVA glue ● old bowl
paintbrush ● brown card ● ruler ● pencil ● scissors
sticky tape ● gouache paints ● wire ● pliers ● pin

1 Put flour, PVA glue and a litttle water into an old bowl and mix into a thick paste.

Blow up a balloon. Cover it with strips of newspaper dipped into the paste. Leave the knot showing.

2 Draw a thick cross on brown card. Draw criss-cross lines on it to look like basketwork.

Cut out the cross. Fold up the sides. Tape the sides together to make a balloon basket.

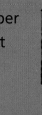 Once the newspaper is dry, cut the knot off the balloon. Paint the paper balloon all over.

Pierce four holes around the base of the balloon and in the corners of the basket, using a pin.

Cut four short pieces of wire with pliers and bend both ends. Hook one end into a hole in the balloon and the other into a hole in the basket.

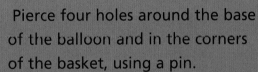

Biplane

thick cardboard roll ● scissors ● 5 corks
white card ● glue ● gouache paints ● paintbrush
ice-lolly stick ● drawing pin

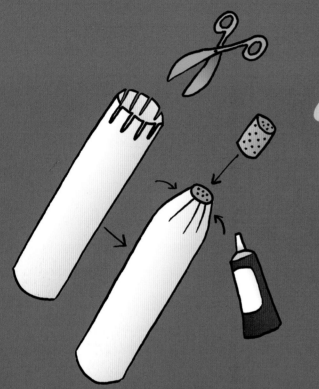

1 Cut little snips all around one end of a cardboard roll. Fit a cork into the roll. Glue the snipped ends around it.

2 Glue two corks together. Repeat with another two corks.

Cut out two wings and three tail fins from white card, in the sizes shown.

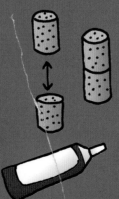

4cm

25cm

3cm

5cm

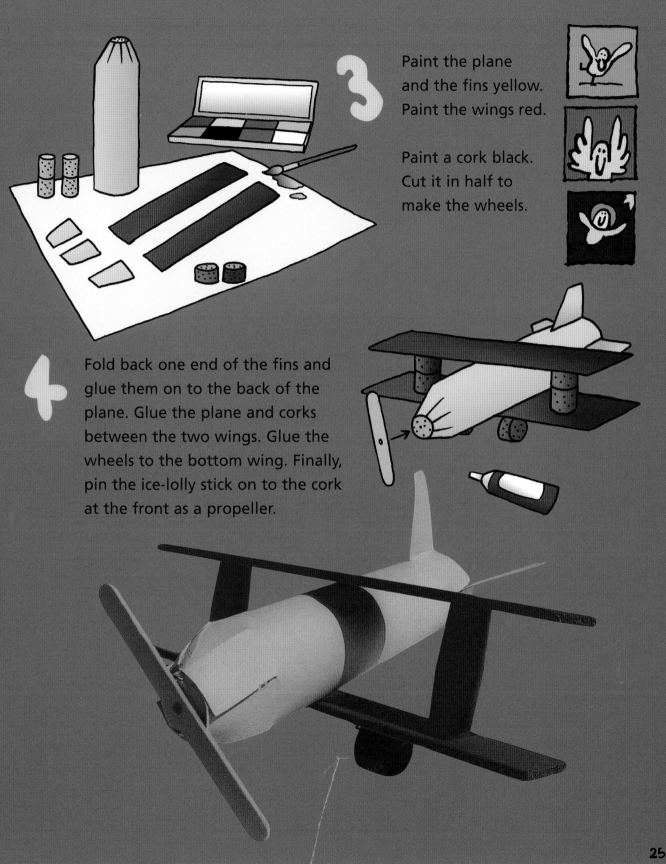

3 Paint the plane and the fins yellow. Paint the wings red.

Paint a cork black. Cut it in half to make the wheels.

4 Fold back one end of the fins and glue them on to the back of the plane. Glue the plane and corks between the two wings. Glue the wheels to the bottom wing. Finally, pin the ice-lolly stick on to the cork at the front as a propeller.

Racing car

cardboard roll ● scissors ● glue ● pencil ● ruler
gouache paints ● paintbrush ● 3 corks ● stiff card
bottle top ● 2 wooden skewers

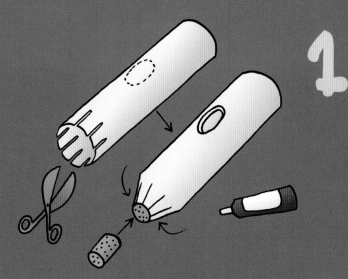

1 Cut little snips around one end of a cardboard roll, and cut a hole in the middle of it.

Fit a cork into the tube and glue the snipped ends around it.

2 Cut four wheels, a tail fin and a square from stiff card, in the sizes shown on the right. Paint the wheels black.

Write a number on the square. Paint the tube and the tail fin both the same colour.

Cut two corks in half. Paint them black.

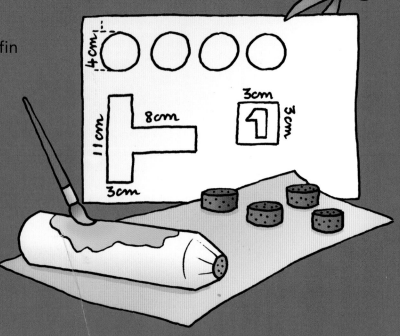

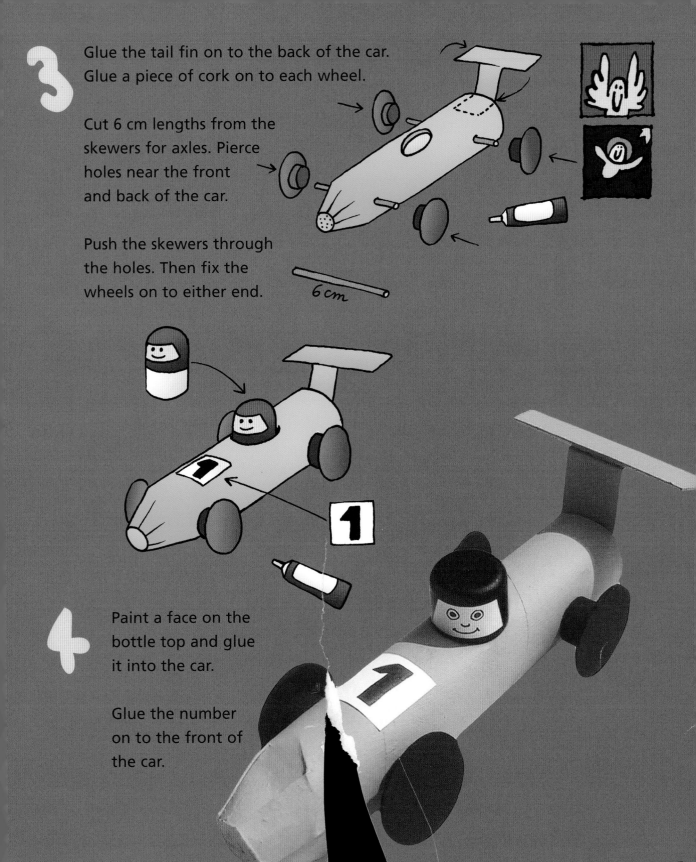

3 Glue the tail fin on to the back of the car. Glue a piece of cork on to each wheel.

Cut 6 cm lengths from the skewers for axles. Pierce holes near the front and back of the car.

Push the skewers through the holes. Then fix the wheels on to either end.

6 cm

4 Paint a face on the bottle top and glue it into the car.

Glue the number on to the front of the car.

Fire engine

empty cereal box or carton ● gouache paint ● paintbrush
stiff white card ● ruler ● pencil ● glue
black felt-tip pen ● string ● scissors

1 Paint a box or carton red all over.

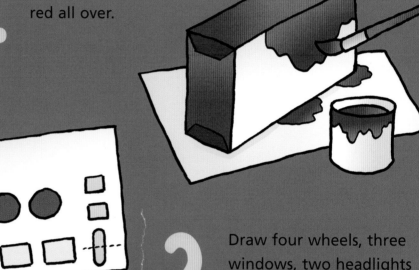

2 Draw four wheels, three windows, two headlights and a hook for the hose from stiff card and size them to fit your box. Cut them out and paint them.

Glue them in place on the fire engine. Draw doors on both sides with a black felt-tip pen.

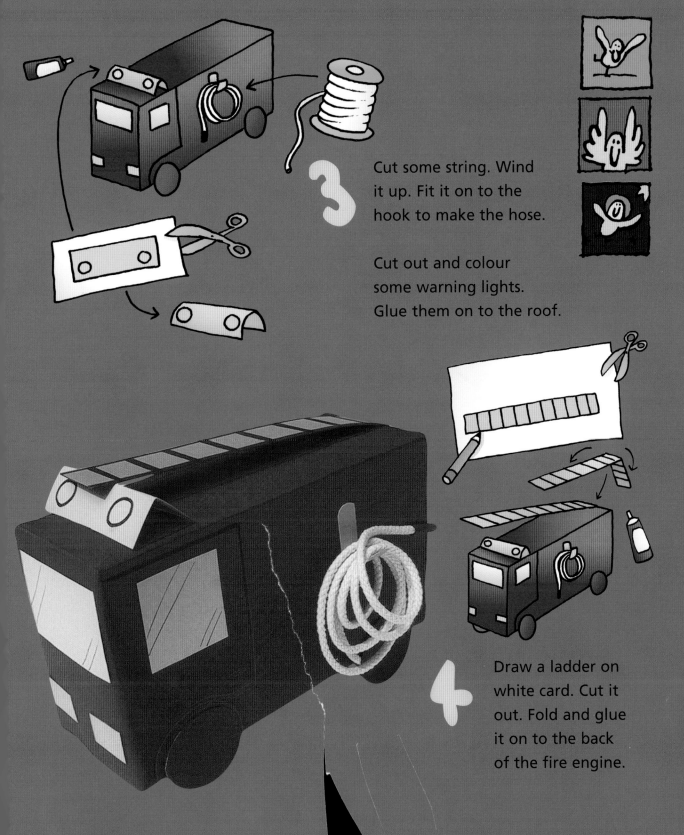

Cut some string. Wind it up. Fit it on to the hook to make the hose.

Cut out and colour some warning lights. Glue them on to the roof.

Draw a ladder on white card. Cut it out. Fold and glue it on to the back of the fire engine.

index